THE WHEEL OF THE TIME

MOIRAINE SEDAI

AATIF WANI

For A. & Kamaljot Kour

Contents

Contents

Acknowledgements

Every reader and lover of Poetry.

    Students, friends, Teachers, Myself: Thanks.

    For Everyone, Anyone, and No-one.

Prologue

Light give me Strength!

"Aes Sedai" means *"Servants of All"*.

It is they who serve the World.

1. I

The World is broken.

Many, many, years ago,

Men who were born with great power believed

That they could cage Darkness itself.

The arrogance.

When they failed, the seas boiled,

Mountains were swallowed up,

Cities burned and destroyed.

And the women of the *Aes Sedai*

Were left to pile up the pieces.

These women remembered

One thing above all else:

The man who brought

The breaking of the World.

And him they named Dragon.

Now, this man has been born again.

We do not know where or to whom.

If he was born as a girl or a boy.

The only thing we know for certain

Is that this Child is coming of age now,

And we must find them before the Darkness does.

2. II

You are a part of me
And I am a part of you.
So, when the Dark surrounds you
And you see no Light,
Feel this that I am a part of you;
And know that I stood before you;
And know that I stand with you.
You are the Wisdom of Ages
And I welcome you to this World.
Be Strong, Trust the God.

3. III

The Wheel of the Time turns,
And Ages come and pass,
Leaving memories that become legend.
Legend fades to myth,
And even myth is long forgotten
When the Age that gave it birth comes again.
In one Age, called the Third Age by someone,
A Wind rose in the Mountain of Mist.
The Wind was not the beginning.
There are neither beginnings nor endings
To the turning of the Wheel of the Time.
But it was a beginning.

4. IV

When I come up here ……
You know what I wonder about?
I wonder about my life here.
About the house I will build.
The wife I will have.
About my kids running
Through these woods, just like I did.
Running through the mist and fog.

5. V

Births and Deaths; Deaths and Births.
No one keeps records of anything.
It does not mean we do not remember.
We remembered.
Until the day we died.
So do I, You, and Everyone.

6. VI

Servants of the Dark.
The Riders of Fade.

7. VII

No one can remember their pervious lives.
All we can do is the best we can
With the life that's given to us.
And take comfort from it.
That no matter what happens,
What pain we face
What heartbreak, even death.
And we try again and again.
Maybe do a little better than the last time.

8. VIII

Words are important,

And how we use them is important.

9. IX

Three Oaths:
One: *To speak no word that is not true.*
Two: *To make no weapon with which*
One person may kill another.
Three: *Never to use the One Power as a weapon,*
Except in the last extreme defence of her life
Or the life of her Warder, or another Aes Sedai.

10. X

The power inside you
Is the smallest part of your strength.
It is your mind and how you use it
That will mean such more in the battles to come.
What do you call it?
This skill that Wisdoms have to predict the weather?
It is the same thing for all of us.
One Thing. One Power.
And like you and I,
We are lucky enough to be able to touch it.
Touching the Source will come to you
Whether you want it to or not.
Look at the Stone.
Look at its surface.
It is clear and opaque
Like the water of a river.
Imagine yourself floating in that river.
As the water moves,
Let it take you. No thoughts.
Just let yourself drift.
Clear your mind of everything.
There are no woods,
There is no hunger,

No exhaustion.
There is only the Stone
And the sound of rushing water.
Let it take you. Surrender.
Let yourself drift. Drift.
You do not listen to the Wind;
It is the Wind that listens to you.

11. XI

Dreams have power.
More than you know.

12. XII

We run if we can,
Endure if we cannot.

13. XIII

Nothing is ever lost.
The Wheel returns all.

14. XIV

Nothing is more dangerous
Then a man who knows the past.

15. XV

'The leaf, in its time,
Falls to the dirt,
That nourishes the tree that,
In its time, grows the leaf again.'

16. XVI

'We lost them.
Twenty years we hunted,
And we lost them.'
'I lost them.'
'Your losses are mine.
And mine yours.'

17. XVII

Always in such a rush,
These humans.
Never taking time to properly prepare
For what they are walking into.

18. XVIII

No decision is still a decision.

19. XIX

You reached out and
You touched the Source.
You will never be the same.

20. XX

Men, women both, once
They've tasted the Power, if
They've cut off from it,
It's no life anymore.

21. XXI

Are the fish stirring?

Aye. Kissing the surface.

Jumping for their breakfast?

Best we catch them, then.

Before some other bastard does.

I'd no more do that than

A fish could touch the moon.

Fish touch the moon's reflection every night.

See? Too bloody clever for this place.

Time to go.

I don't belong there.

At the White Tower.

I should be here with you.

Look at me.

You're gonna do great things.

And if any of them bastards

Tries to shame you,

You show them who you are:

"Daughter of the river.

Clever as a pike.

Strong as the tides."

22. XXII

'*Moiraine* has flitted back and forth
To the Tower for 20 years.
Her purpose: the purpose of all Blues:
Is to gather Secrets
And discover danger
Before it strikes at the heart of us,
Before it strikes at you.
But *Trollocs* invaded from the west,
Without even a warning from *Moiraine*.'
'What is the purpose of your travels?'
'I cannot say.
Cannot… or will not?
You dare to challenge me?
Perhaps it is your noble blood,
Lady Moiraine Damadred,
That breeds contempt for those
You consider beneath you.
Outside this Tower, it seems
You do as you please.
But I am the *Amyrlin Seat*.
This is my Tower.
My City. My World.
From Tear to the Two Rivers

And every town between.
Remember that well
While you are here.
Remember that well
When your forehead
And your lips touch this marble
And you beg me for mercy!
'Swear your oath, *Moiraine Sedai*,
Before all, in this Sacred Hall.
The One Power renders it unbreakable
And eternally binding.
By the Light and my hope
Of Salvation and Rebirth
I, *Moiraine Sedai*, swear
To obey the judgment
Of the *Amyrlin Seat*
And never return till she calls me home,
Or may the Creator's face turn from me
And Darkness consumes my soul.'
'By the Light and the hope
Of my Salvation and Rebirth
I, *Moiraine Sedai*, do swear
To honour and obey *Siuan Sanche*
Daughter of the River
Clever as a pike
Strong as the tides
And never return until

She calls me home,

Or may my Creator's face turn from me

And Darkness consumes my soul.'

23. XXIII

The Wheel weaves
As the Wheel wills.
There's no turning back.
Whatever happens now
Is beyond our control.

This is not The END.